I AM NOT A CEREAL BOX

THE RECYCLING PROJECT BOOK

10 EXCITING THINGS TO MAKE WITH CEREAL BOXES!

First edition for North America published in 2018
by Barron's Educational Series, Inc.

Text and design copyright © 2018 Carlton Books Limited

Published in 2018 by Carlton Books Limited, an imprint of the
Carlton Publishing Group, 20 Mortimer Street, London W1T 3JW

All inquiries should be addressed to:
Barron's Educational Series, Inc.
250 Wireless Boulevard
Hauppauge, NY 11788
www.barronseduc.com

ISBN: 978-1-4380-1242-1
Library of Congress Control
Number: 2018941667

Date of Manufacture: July 2018
Manufactured by: RRD Asia, Kowloon,
Hong Kong

Printed in China
9 8 7 6 5 4 3 2 1

Creative Director: Clare Baggaley
Written, designed, illustrated, and packaged by: Dynamo Limited

I AM NOT A CEREAL BOX

THE RECYCLING PROJECT BOOK

BARRON'S

10 EXCITING THINGS TO MAKE WITH CEREAL BOXES!

Hi THERE!

ARE YOU READY TO GET STARTED? OF COURSE YOU ARE!

THIS CRAFT BOOK IS FULL OF PROJECTS THAT YOU CAN MAKE WITH JUST A CEREAL BOX AND A FEW BITS AND PIECES! USE YOUR IMAGINATION AND FOLLOW THE STEP-BY-STEP GUIDES TO CREATE YOUR CRAFTS.

IF YOU'D LIKE, YOU CAN USE THE HANDY CUTOUTS AT THE BACK OF THIS BOOK TO HELP YOU.

YOU WILL NEED

- LOTS OF CEREAL BOXES
- A MIX OF CARDBOARD TUBES AND SCRAPS OF CARDSTOCK
- TIN FOIL
- PAINTS
- PAINTBRUSHES
- BOTTLE CAPS
- BUTTONS
- YARN
- SEQUINS
- PIPE CLEANERS
- TAPE
- GLUE
- SAFETY SCISSORS

YOU'LL NEED A GROWN-UP TO HELP YOU WITH ALL OF THESE PROJECTS!

CONTENTS

5

ROBOT!

I AM A ROBOT AND BEING SMART IS MY MIDDLE NAME! I'M MADE FROM THE VERY BEST **TECHNOLOGY** AROUND, YOU SEE, NOT JUST SOME SILLY OLD CARDBOARD BOX!

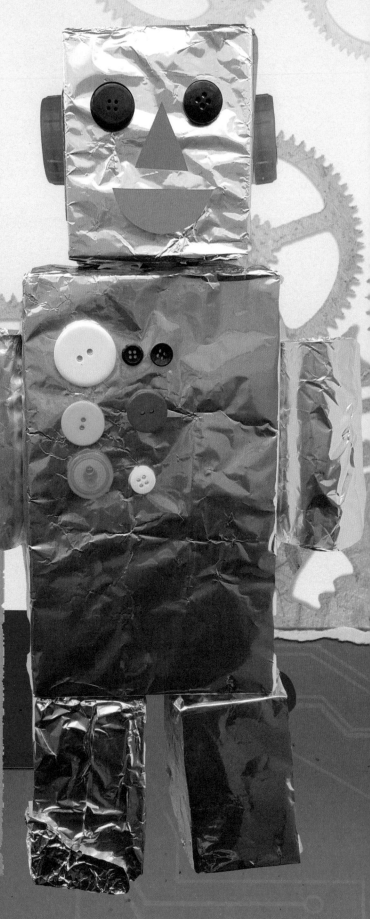

YOU WILL NEED

- ONE BIG CEREAL BOX
- THREE MINI CEREAL BOXES
- TIN FOIL
- OAKTAG
- CARDBOARD TUBES
- TAPE
- BUTTONS AND BOTTLE CAPS
- GLUE
- COLORFUL PAPER
- SAFETY SCISSORS

SET THE SCENE

Make your robot feel at home by creating a techno-fabulous background for it to stand in. Draw cogs, wheels, and buttons onto a big piece of oaktag and use pencils, pens, or gray paint to fill them in. Use pieces of tin foil to build up texture and add extra shine. Turn the page to find out how to make your own nifty robot buddy.

DID YOU KNOW? LEONARDO DA VINCI CAME UP WITH PLANS FOR A ROBOT IN THE LATE 1400s!

DO THE ROBOT DANCE!

GO FURTHER!

IF A WHOLE ROBOT IS A BIT TOO MUCH FOR YOU, WHY NOT MAKE A GIANT ROBOT HEAD INSTEAD? JUST TURN THE PAGE TO FIND OUT HOW.

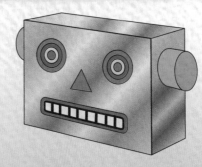

I'M A ROBOT!

1

Cover your big and small cereal boxes in tin foil; then, tape the small box on top of the big box to make a robot head and body.

2

For the arms, cover two toilet paper or kitchen roll tubes in tin foil and tape them to each side of the body, like this. If you don't have spare tubes, you could make your own by rolling pieces of cardstock and taping them in place.

3

For the legs, cover two more small cereal boxes in tin foil. Turn them sideways and tape them to the bottom of your robot body.

4

Glue bottle caps on each side of the head for ears, then glue or tape on buttons for eyes.

5

Cut a triangle and semi-circle out of red paper to make a nose and a mouth for your robot. Glue or tape these on to make a friendly face.

6

Finally, give your robot lots of dials and knobs using spare buttons and bottle caps. You could even give him a different mouth. Get creative!

I AM NOT A CEREAL BOX...
I'M A GIANT ROBOT HEAD!

To make your huge robot face, turn your large cereal box on its side and cover it in colorful paper or tin foil. Draw around a cup onto colorful paper to make two large eyes, then make a triangle nose and rectangle mouth shapes, too. Use white paper or stickers for teeth and cut small sections of a toilet paper roll for ears, too!

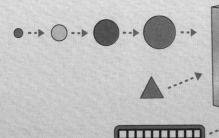

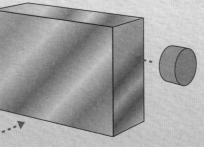

AQUARIUM!

CHECK OUT ALL OF MY **TROPICAL FISH** AND MY **COLORFUL CORAL REEF!** AS YOU CAN SEE, I AM AN AQUARIUM, SO WHY DON'T YOU LOOK INSIDE TO SPOT ALL THE **EXCITING CREATURES?**

YOU WILL NEED

- ONE CEREAL BOX
- PAINTS
- PAINTBRUSHES
- TISSUE PAPER
- PIPE CLEANERS
- GLUE
- OAKTAG
- CARDSTOCK
- SAFETY SCISSORS
- SEQUINS AND GLITTER
- GOOGLY EYES
- THREAD
- TAPE

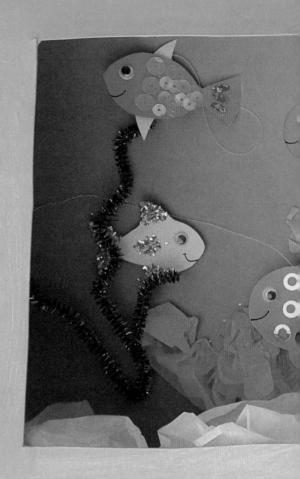

SET THE SCENE

Give your aquarium a watery feel by tearing up strips of blue tissue paper and taping them to a piece of oaktag. Paint on colorful coral or seaweed for a dash of color. Turn the page to find out how to transform your cereal box into an underwater world full of color and fishy friends.

DID YOU KNOW?
FISH WERE ON THE PLANET BEFORE DINOSAURS!

SPLISH, SPLASH, SPLOSH!

GO FURTHER!

YOU CAN MAKE DIFFERENT BACKGROUNDS TO SLOT INSIDE YOUR AQUARIUM. LET'S FIND OUT HOW OVER ON THE NEXT PAGE!

I'M AN AQUARIUM

1

Carefully cut away a rectangle from the front of your cereal box. Paint the inside of your box blue first, then pick a color to paint the outside. Leave this to dry while you complete Step 2.

2

Tear strips of colorful tissue paper and scrunch them up to look like coral. Bend pipe cleaners to create sea plants. Once your aquarium scene is dry, glue them to the blue background.

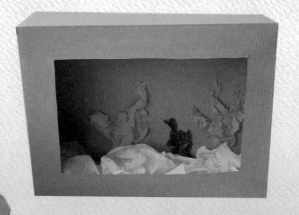

3

Next, scrunch up some yellow tissue paper and place it in the bottom of your box to mimic sand, as shown. Now your aquarium is taking shape!

4

Cut out lots of fish from cardstock in different shapes, colors, and sizes.

5

Have fun decorating your fish with sequins, glitter, and paints. Don't forget to add your googly eyes from this book!

6

Stick some fish to your background and tape the rest to pieces of thread. Tape the thread to the top of the cereal box to make your fish float. There are a couple of fish cutouts at the back of this book to get you started.

I AM NOT A CEREAL BOX...

I'M AN UNDERWATER SCENE

Make your aquarium even more awesome by creating different background scenes. Find a piece of cardstock that fits inside the box and get creative! How about drawing a shipwreck, pretty mermaids, or even some crazy deep sea monsters! The choice is yours. And cut out other sea creatures such as an octopus or sea horse to hang in front.

CAR!

BEEP, BEEP! HERE I COME, ZOOMING ALONG TO CARRY YOUR LUCKY TEDDY BEAR ON EXCITING ADVENTURES AROUND THE HOUSE. WHICH FURRY FRIENDS WILL YOU CHOOSE TO GO FOR A SPIN?

YOU WILL NEED

- ONE CEREAL BOX
- PAINTS
- PAINTBRUSHES
- SAFETY SCISSORS
- COLORFUL PAPER
- GLUE
- TIN FOIL
- CARDSTOCK
- TAPE

VROOOM VROOOM!

14

SET THE SCENE

Paint sheets of cardstock with a white stripe down the middle to make a highway for your car to drive along. When the paint dries, tape the sheets together to make a road. Go one step further and cut out road signs and traffic lights from colorful paper to pop along the road, too! Look at the next page to find out how to turn an old cereal box into a cool new car for your favorite teddy bear to ride around in.

DID YOU KNOW?
THE FIRST CAR WAS INVENTED BY KARL BENZ FROM GERMANY.

GO FURTHER!

IF YOU WANT A VEHICLE WITH ROOM FOR ALL OF YOUR TOYS TO RIDE IN, WE HAVE AN IDEA FOR YOU ON THE NEXT PAGE.

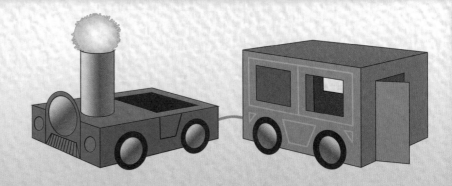

I'M A CAR!

1

First, paint your cereal box all over in any color you like. When the paint is completely dry, carefully cut out a square shape from the top of the cereal box. Make sure it's big enough to fit your teddy bear in.

2

For headlights, cut out two yellow paper circles and paint a black dot on each. Glue these to the front of your car.

3

Now, cut a rectangle out of tin foil to glue on the front of your car in the middle of the headlights.

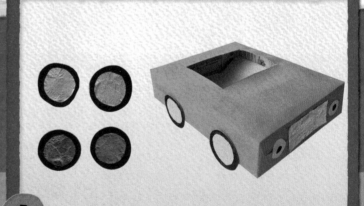

4

Cut out 4 wheels from black cardstock. You could add a circle of tin foil to each wheel to look like a hubcap! Glue your wheels in place.

5

Cut a steering wheel out of black cardstock and tape it so that it pokes out from the middle square section of your car.

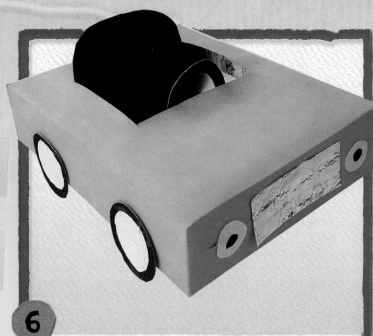

6

Finally, snip out a curved piece of black cardstock to make the back of the seat for your teddy bear driver! Simply tape it in place and your car is ready.

I AM NOT A CEREAL BOX...
I'M A TRAIN!

Turn your car into a terrific train by painting lots of boxes and joining them together using string and tape. Don't forget to add a funnel to the front of your train by rolling up a piece of cardstock or using a toilet paper roll. *Toot, toot!*

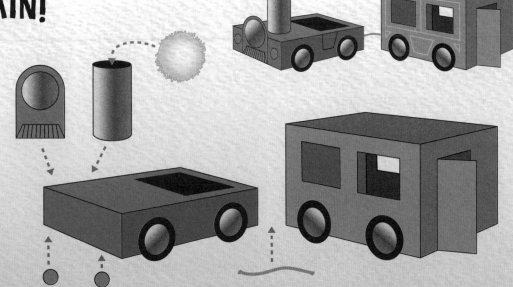

DINOSAURRRRR!

I'M A GREAT BIG **DINO**, CAN'T YOU SEE? I'M FAR TOO **FIERCE** TO BE A CEREAL BOX. YOU WILL KNOW IT'S ME WHEN I OPEN MY HUGE JAW AND

ROAR, ROAR, ROAR!

YOU WILL NEED

- ONE CEREAL BOX
- SAFETY SCISSORS
- CARDSTOCK
- GLUE
- GREEN AND BLACK PAINT
- WHITE CARDSTOCK
- YELLOW CARDSTOCK
- TAPE

SET THE SCENE

Create a whole land for your dino to explore! Scrunch up magazines or newspapers to make big boulders and rocks for your prehistoric pal to stomp through. You could cut out big dino footprints from paper and lay them around your room. Make your own tooth-tastic dino hat to bring this cereal box to life. Turn the page to find out how!

DID YOU KNOW?
DINOSAURS ROAMED THE PLANET FOR 165 MILLION YEARS IN THE MESOZOIC ERA.

ROOAAAAR!

GO FURTHER!

DO YOU LOVE HORSES? WELL, YOU CAN MAKE ONE OF THOSE TOO! TURN THE PAGE TO FOLLOW OUR EASY STEP-BY-STEP GUIDE.

I'M A DINOSAUR!

1

Carefully cut a hole out of the front of your cereal box. It will need to be big enough to fit the top of your head comfortably. Turn the cereal box over so that the hole is underneath.

2

Cut two eye shapes, like this, out of cardstock and tape these onto your cereal box. Paint it green all over and leave to dry.

3

Make some beady eyes by painting big black dots onto white circles of paper. Stick these onto your dino, then glue on triangles cut out of white cardstock to make pointy teeth.

4

Next, paint on two black nostrils. You can also finger paint yellow splotches all over your dino to look like scales! Leave this to dry.

5 Cut out a strip of zigzags from yellow cardstock.

6 Tape on the zigzag strip so that it sits in the middle of your dino's eyes, like this, and you're all done! Place your new pal on top of your head and transform yourself into a roaring dinosaur!

I AM NOT A CEREAL BOX...
I'M A HORSE'S HEAD!

To make a horse's head, just turn the box on its side and cut out a mouth as shown. Stick in a red tongue and add two ears and eyes. Finally, give your horse a mane made of yarn.

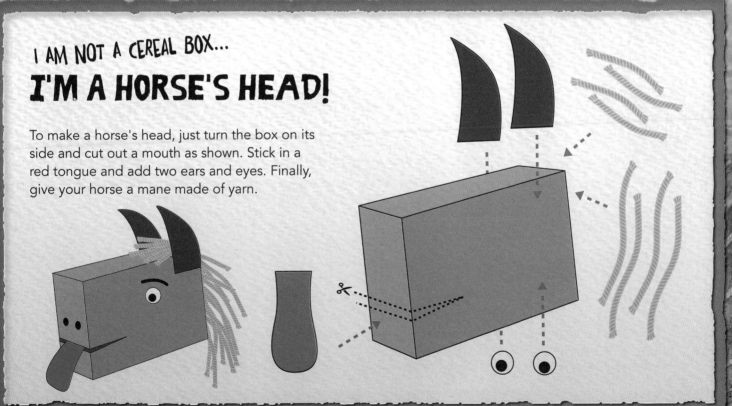

CASTLE!

A CEREAL BOX COULD NEVER LOOK AS GRAND AS ME BECAUSE I AM A CASTLE. I STAND TALL AND PROUD IN THE COUNTRYSIDE WITH MY FLAGS FLYING IN THE WIND! MY DRAWBRIDGE MOVES UP AND DOWN TO KEEP EVERYONE SAFE INSIDE.

YOU WILL NEED

- ONE CEREAL BOX
- SAFETY SCISSORS
- 4 TOILET PAPER ROLLS
- PAINTS
- PAINTBRUSHES
- TAPE
- CARDSTOCK
- STRING
- COLORFUL PAPER
- LOLLIPOP STICKS
- GLUE

COME AND EXPLORE!

SET THE SCENE

Tear strips of green paper to collage a beautiful countryside background. Cut a circle of blue paper to make a moat for your castle to sit on, too. Turn the page to find out how to make your own castle.

DID YOU KNOW? WINDSOR CASTLE IN BRITAIN HAS AROUND 1,000 ROOMS!

GO FURTHER!

MAKE YOUR CASTLE THE MOST MAGNIFICENT IN ALL THE LAND BY BUILDING A WHOLE FORTRESS! WANT TO KNOW HOW? JUST TURN THE PAGE AND YOU WILL SEE!

I'M A CASTLE!

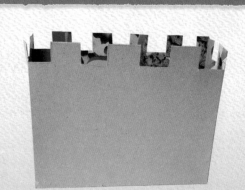

1

First, cut little rectangles out of one side of your cereal box to make fortifications.

2

Take four toilet paper roll tubes and cut little turrets into the top of each one. If you don't have toilet paper rolls, make your own tubes by rolling cardstock and taping it together. Now paint everything orange.

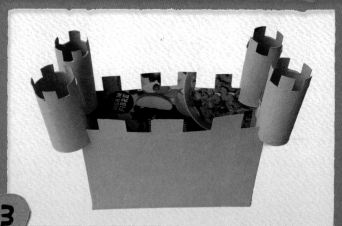

3

Cut two slits (about 3/4 in [2 cm]) in the bottom of each toilet paper roll so that they can hook onto the main body of the castle. Tape each turret to a corner of your castle to keep it in place.

4

Cut some flag shapes from colorful paper and tape them to lollipop sticks. Then, tape the sticks to the inside of each turret.

5

Cut an archway shape out of red cardstock and glue it to your castle. To make a drawbridge, cut a rectangle from cardstock. Make two holes in the top of the cardstock and two more on either side of the door. Thread string through each side as shown and tie a knot in each end to keep it in place.

6

Finally, paint some windows onto the front of your castle and test the drawbridge!

I AM NOT A CEREAL BOX...
I'M A CASTLE CITY!

Keep adding to your castle to make a fortress! Find more cereal boxes, or other unwanted boxes, to decorate and turn them into castles. Next, join each castle together by making battlements out of long boxes or strips of cardstock.

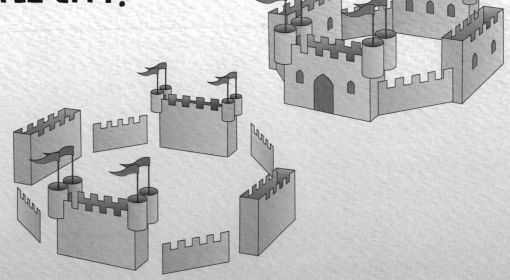

ELEPHAAAANT!

I AM AN ENORMOUS ELEPHANT AND I'M A GIANT OF THE JUNGLE! SUNSHINE, SWIMMING, AND PLENTY OF MUD BATHS ARE MY FAVORITE THINGS.

YOU WILL NEED

- ONE CEREAL BOX
- PINK, GRAY, BLACK, AND WHITE PAINT
- PAINTBRUSHES
- WHITE CARDSTOCK
- SAFETY SCISSORS
- GLUE
- TAPE

SET THE SCENE

Get your pens and pencils ready to create your own jungle scene to stand behind your cereal box elephant. What kinds of trees will you draw? You could even doodle lots of yummy bananas and grass for your elephant to chomp on. Turn the page to learn how to make your cardboard king of the jungle.

ANYONE FANCY A WATER FIGHT?

DID YOU KNOW?
ELEPHANTS EAT FRUITS, PLANTS, AND GRASS. THEY ESPECIALLY LOVE BANANAS!

GO FURTHER!

ELEPHANTS AREN'T THE ONLY ANIMALS YOU CAN MAKE FROM CEREAL BOXES. WHY NOT TRY THIS CUTE PIG NEXT?

I'M AN ELEPHANT!

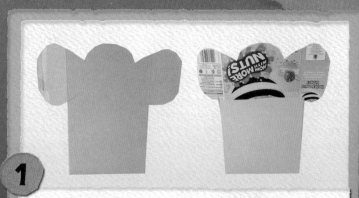

1

Carefully cut your cereal box so that the front section looks like two flappy elephant ears. The back of the box should still stand up, just like the second picture above.

2

To make legs, cut an archway shape out of the front of your cereal box. Then, turn over your box and cut out the same shape for the back legs.

3

Use the leftover part of the cereal box to make a trunk. Simply cut out a thin rectangle and tape it in place.

4

Next, paint your elephant pink all over and leave it to dry.

5

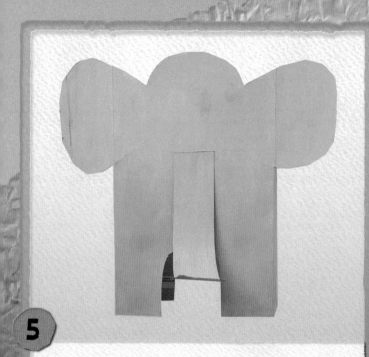

Then, cut some white triangle tusks out of cardstock and glue them to each side of the trunk.

6

All that's left to do is to glue on some eyes made out of white circles, paint on some details, and add toenails.

I AM NOT A CEREAL BOX...
I'M A PIG!

Turn your box on its side and cut out rectangles like those shown to make four legs. Paint the box pink and cut out a big circle of pink cardstock, then stick on the circle for the face. Add a curly pipe cleaner tail and glue on ears, eyes, and a piggy snout. *Oink oink!*

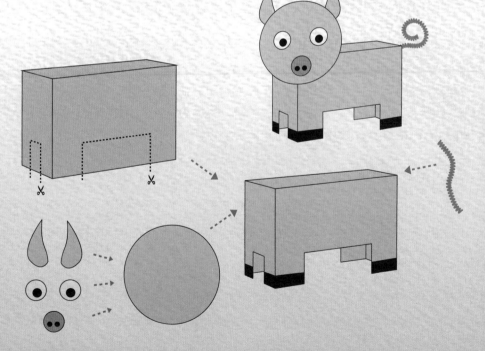

ROCK STAR GUITAR!

LET'S RAISE THE ROOF! I AM A ROCK STAR GUITAR THAT ALWAYS PUTS ON A SHOW. TUNE IN YOUR EARS BECAUSE I'M READY FOR MY BIG SOLO!

YOU WILL NEED

- ONE CEREAL BOX
- SAFETY SCISSORS
- PAINTS
- PAINTBRUSHES
- LONG CARDBOARD TUBE
- PIPE CLEANERS
- TAPE
- YARN
- BLACK CARDSTOCK
- COLORFUL PAPER TO DECORATE

SET THE SCENE

Make stage lights for your music show! Paint some empty, clean yogurt containers and when they're dry, tape different colors of bright tissue paper over the ends of them. You could tape a few containers together to make a row of disco lights. Make a cereal box's dreams of fame come true and turn it into a rock star guitar. Our step-by-step guide is on the next page.

TWANG TWAAANG!

DID YOU KNOW?
GUITARS USUALLY HAVE SIX STRINGS, BUT FOUR- AND TWELVE-STRING VERSIONS ARE POPULAR TOO! YOU CAN EVEN FIND SEVEN-, EIGHT-, NINE-, AND TEN-STRING VERSIONS.

GO FURTHER!

COMPLETE YOUR BAND BY MAKING A DRUM SO YOUR FRIENDS CAN JOIN IN WITH YOU! TURN THE PAGE AND WE WILL SHOW YOU HOW.

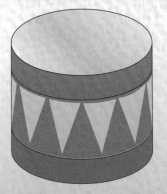

I'M A ROCK GUITAR!

1

Carefully cut a circle out of the front of your cereal box. Then choose a bright color to paint all over and leave to dry.

2

Next, paint your cardboard tube in a different color. When it's dry, cut some pipe cleaners to 1$\frac{1}{2}$ in (4 cm) and tape them to the end.

3

Tuck the lid of the cereal box down to make a space, then push your long tube through. Tape it in place as shown.

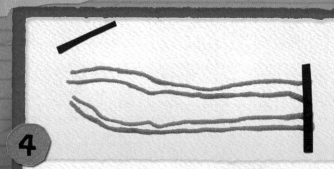

4

Use yarn to make guitar strings. Make the yarn long enough to reach across the cereal box. Tape the ends of the string to a piece of black cardstock, like this.

5

Now tape the strings to your guitar so that they go across the center of the hole you made.

6

Finally, decorate your guitar with a fun design and get ready to rock out!

I AM NOT A CEREAL BOX...
I'M A DRUM!

Did you know it's easy to turn a rectangular cereal box into a round drum? Use the instructions here to draw a plan on a flattened box. Cut all the pieces out and stick them together with tape as shown. Stick a couple of corks onto the end of drinking straws to make drumsticks.

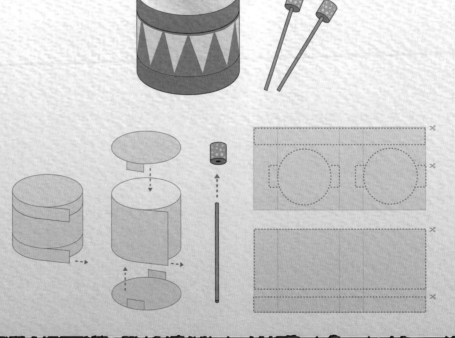

BUILDING!

I'M A **HUGE BUILDING** STRETCHING WAY UP **INTO THE CLOUDS!** I'M HAPPIEST IN THE **CITY** WITH ALL THE OTHER **SKYSCRAPERS STANDING TALL.**

YOU WILL NEED
- ONE CEREAL BOX
- PAINTS
- PAINTBRUSHES
- SAFETY SCISSORS

SET THE SCENE

Make a background scene for your skyscraper to stand in. Draw and color an exciting skyline full of different-shaped buildings. Don't forget to finish the scene with a bright blue sky. Try adding fluffy clouds or even a rainbow. Turn the page to start making your own building.

THERE ARE GREAT VIEWS UP HERE!

DID YOU KNOW? THE TALLEST BUILDING IN THE WORLD IS THE BURJ KHALIFA IN DUBAI, WHICH IS 2,722 FT (829.8 M) HIGH!

GO FURTHER!

WHY STOP AT ONE BUILDING? TURN TO THE NEXT PAGE FOR IDEAS ON HOW TO MAKE A WHOLE CITY.

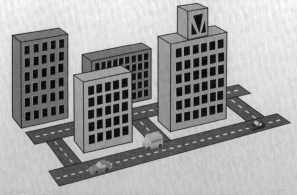

I'M A BUILDING!

1

Paint your cereal box in a nice bright color and leave it to dry. Now it's time to paint on your windows! Use a darker color to paint rows of rectangles onto your box until it looks like this, and then leave it to dry.

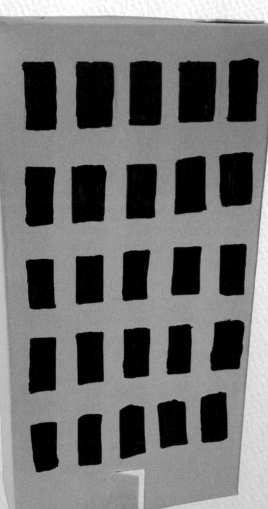

2

To make a door, cut three sides of a rectangle into the bottom of your cereal box. Fold this back to create a door that you can open and close.

3

If you like, you could try cutting the top and bottom of a rectangle with a cut down in the middle to make double doors. Also, try different-shaped boxes and paint them in different colors!

I AM NOT A CEREAL BOX...
I'M A WHOLE CITY!

Paint a variety of different cereal boxes to make lots of buildings. Then lay out all of your fabulous buildings on a flat surface and cut out rectangles of black paper to make roads. Now your toy cars can drive around your new city!

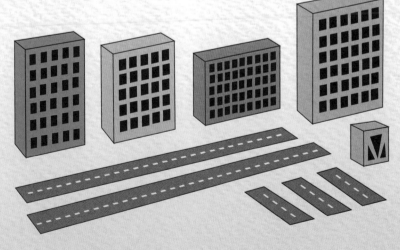

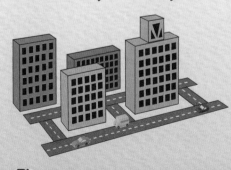

MARBLE RUN!

WOULD YOU LIKE TO RACE? I AM A **MARVELOUS** MARBLE RUN FULL OF **SLOPES AND RAMPS** TO RACE FROM THE TOP ALL THE WAY DOWN.

READY, SET,... GO!

YOU WILL NEED
- ONE CEREAL BOX
- PAINTS
- PAINTBRUSHES
- SAFETY SCISSORS
- TAPE

SET THE SCENE

Why not turn your marble run into a fairground stall? Make signs saying "Take a chance!" and "Marvelous marble run!" and then set your stall up on a small table. Now, turn the page and learn how to make your fun-tastic marble run.

GO FURTHER!

YOU CAN ALSO MAKE A MEGA MAZE FOR YOUR MARBLES TO ZOOM AROUND. TURN THE PAGE AND ALL WILL BE REVEALED!

DID YOU KNOW?
THE LONGEST MARBLE RUN MEASURES 9,376 FT (2,858 M)!

ROLL WITH IT!

I'M A MARBLE RUN!

1

Carefully cut the front of your cereal box away so it looks like this. Keep the leftover cereal box safe as you will need it in Step 3.

2

Paint the inside of your marble run with a bright color paint and leave it to dry.

3

To make the paths for your marbles to roll down, cut your leftover cereal box into four strips. Paint them in bright colors and leave them to dry.

4

Fold the end of each strip, like this.

5 Use the fold to tape each strip to the inside of your cereal box to make a sloped path. Tape each path on alternate sides and keep going until the path leads all the way to the bottom.

6 Now decorate your marble run by finger painting colorful polka dots on the background.

I AM NOT A CEREAL BOX...
I'M A MARBLE MAZE!

Complete Step 1 as shown, then lay your cereal box down flat. Build a maze path using strips of colorful cardstock and tape them in place. You can make your maze as tricky as you like by creating dead ends and lots of twists and turns. To play, gently tip your maze from side to side.

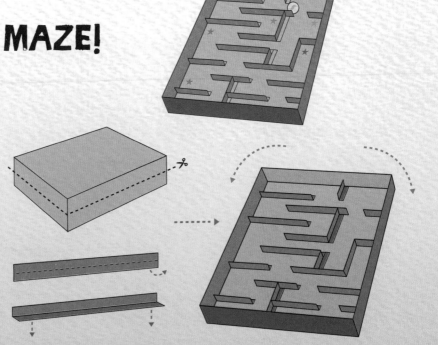

PUPPET THEATER!

COME ONE, COME ALL! THERE'S A NEW SHOW IN TOWN, SO GET YOUR TICKETS FOR THE OPENING NIGHT. TAKE YOUR SEATS. WILL IT BE A COMEDY, A DRAMA, PERHAPS, OR EVEN A MYSTERY!

YOU WILL NEED

- ONE CEREAL BOX
- SAFETY SCISSORS
- PAINT
- PAINTBRUSHES
- TISSUE PAPER
- YARN OR STRING
- TAPE
- RED PAPER
- STARS & GLITTER

THAT'S SHOW BUSINESS!

SET THE SCENE

Why not make theater tickets to give to your friends and family? Cut some rectangles out of paper, write on the name and time of your show, and decorate them. Put on a sell-out performance with your very own puppet theater and turn the page to find out how!

DID YOU KNOW? PUPPETS COME IN ALL SHAPES AND SIZES! SOME ARE FLUFFY AND CUTE, AND SOME ARE REALISTIC, LIKE E.T.!

GO FURTHER!

MAKE YOUR OWN PUPPETS TO PERFORM IN YOUR THEATER! TURN THE PAGE TO FIND OUT HOW!

I'M A PUPPET THEATER!

1 First, carefully cut away a big rectangle from the front and back of your cereal box. Then, paint it all over and leave it to dry.

2 Fold a long strip of tissue paper to make pleats, as shown—these will make your theater curtains.

3 Tape a curtain to each side of the stage.

4 Use yarn or string to make curtain ties.

5

Tape on semi-circles of red paper along the top of the stage to complete your curtains.

6

Decorate your theater using paper stars and gold glitter. Now all you need are the puppets!

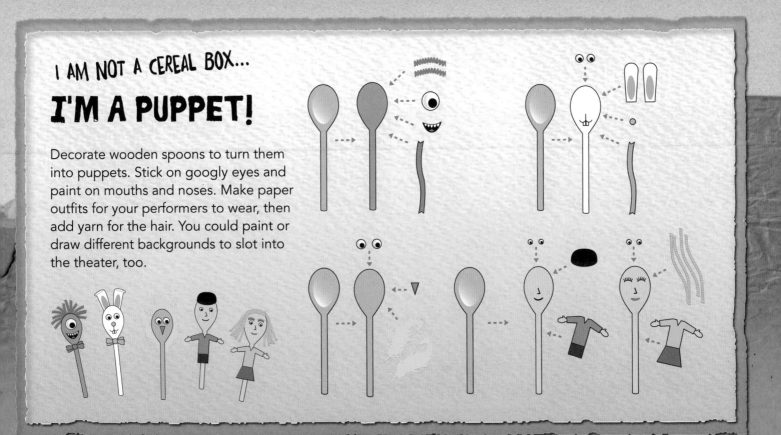

I AM NOT A CEREAL BOX...
I'M A PUPPET!

Decorate wooden spoons to turn them into puppets. Stick on googly eyes and paint on mouths and noses. Make paper outfits for your performers to wear, then add yarn for the hair. You could paint or draw different backgrounds to slot into the theater, too.

YOUR DESIGNS

NOW IT'S OVER TO YOU... THE ONLY THING HOLDING YOUR EMPTY CEREAL BOXES BACK FROM GREATNESS IS YOUR OWN IMAGINATION! SKETCH YOUR IDEAS HERE—WE'VE GIVEN YOU A COUPLE OF BOXES TO GET YOU STARTED.

Robot smile

Elephant tusks

Dinosaur zigzag

Robot nose

Robot teeth

Car headlights

Car steering wheel

Aquarium fish

Car seat

Castle flags

Castle windows

Castle door